HOME ORGANIST LIBRARY VOLUME 9

Beatles Songs

Wise Publications
London/New York/Sydney/Cologne

£4.95

Exclusive Distributors:
Music Sales Limited
8/9 Frith Street, London W1V 5TZ, England
Music Sales Pty. Limited
27 Clarendon Street, Artarmon, Sydney, NSW 2064, Australia

ISBN 0.86001.970.5
Order No. NO 18186

Designed by Howard Brown/John Gorham
Cover photograph by Tony Evans

Printed and bound in England by
Anchor Brendon Limited, Tiptree, Essex.

Contents

All My Loving

Words & Music: John Lennon & Paul McCartney

SUGGESTED REGISTRATIONS

Electronic Organs	Drawbar Organs
Upper: Flute 8', 4' String 8'	Upper: 43 8070 604
Lower: Diapason 8' French Horn 8'	Pedal: 5-(4)
Pedal: 16'+8'	Vibrato: On
Vibrato: On	

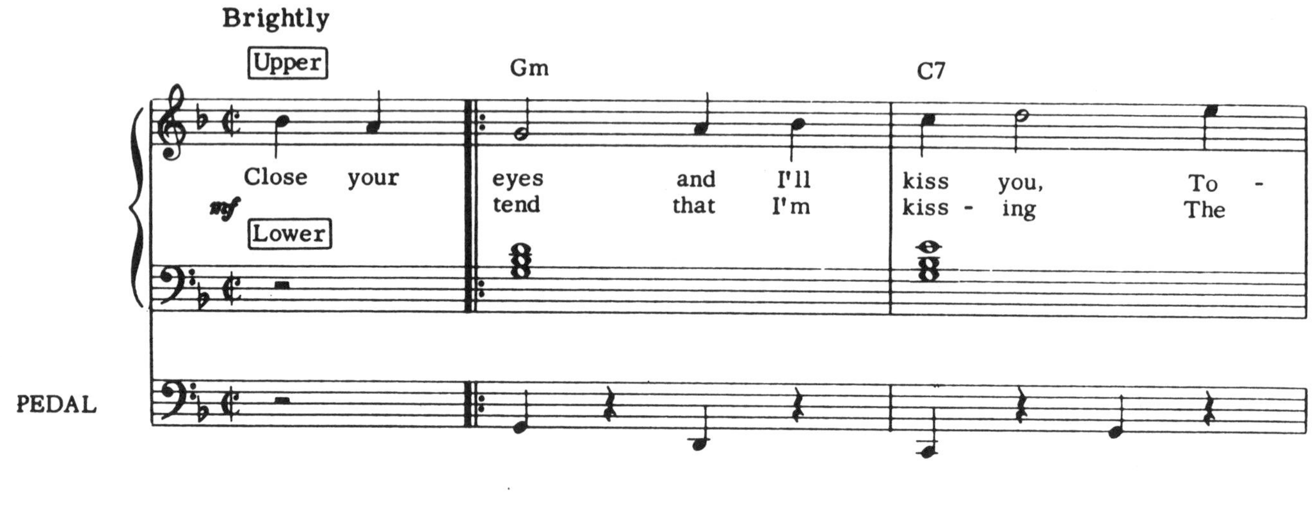

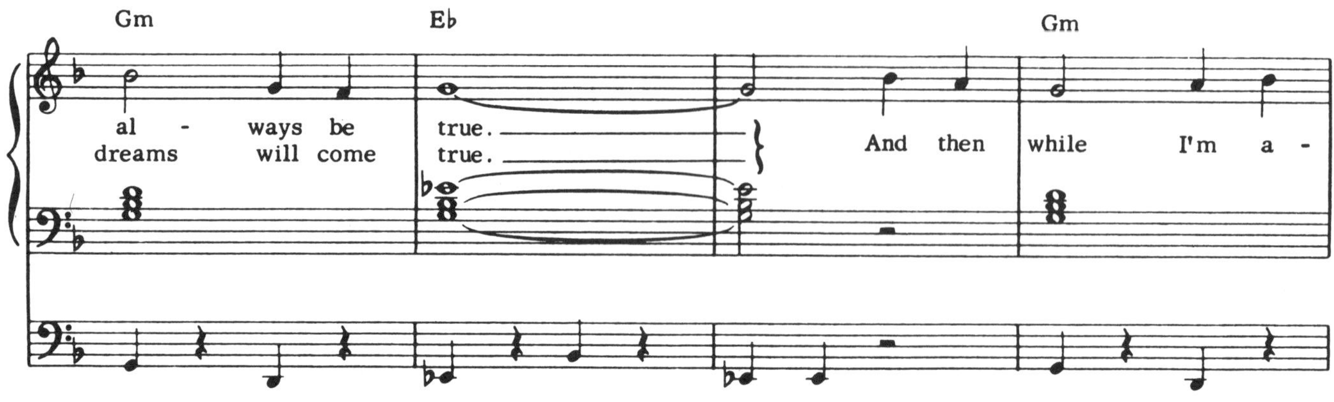

C7
F
Dm
B♭
way, I'll write home ev - 'ry day, And I'll send all my
C7
F
1.
2.
F
lov - ing to you. 2. I'll pre - All my
Dm
F+
F
lov - ing I will send to you, All my
Dm
F+
F
lov - ing, dar - ling, I'll be true.

I Feel Fine

Words & Music: John Lennon & Paul McCartney

SUGGESTED REGISTRATIONS

Electronic Organs		Drawbar Organs	
Upper:	Flute 16' (Or 8') Fl. 2', Piccolo 2'	Upper:	60 7600 220 (0)
Lower:	String 8' Diapason 8'	Lower:	(00) 5544 220 (0)
Pedal:	8	Pedal:	4-(2)
Vibrato:	On	Vibrato:	On

Moderate beat

Eb
Eb
I'm so
Gm
Ab
Bb7
glad that she's my lit - tle girl,
Eb
Gm
Fm7
She's so glad she's tell - ing all the
Bb7
D.C. al Coda
world, (3.) That her
CODA
E

When I'm Sixty Four

Words & Music: John Lennon & Paul McCartney

SUGGESTED REGISTRATIONS

Electronic Organs	Drawbar Organs
Upper: Flute 16', 8' 4' Quint, Nazard	Upper: 70 8623 001
Lower: Flute 8', 4', Diapason 8'	Lower: (00) 6433 322 (0)
Pedal: 8'	Pedal: 5-(3)
Vibrato: On	Vibrato: On

C7
F
quar - ter to three
would you lock the
door
dig - ging the weeds
who could ask for
more
fill in a form
mine for ev - er
more
F6
Ab7
C6
A7
D7
G7
To Coda
C
Will you still need me,
will you still feed me,
when I'm six - ty
four
Am
G
1. (Tacet)
oo
2. Ev-'ry sum-mer we can rent a
cot - tage in the Isle of
Wight if it's not too
Am
G
F
dear
You'll be
old - er
(Ah
We shall
scrimp and
(We shall scrimp and

E7
too
save
save)
Am Em7
Ah
Ah
Am Em7
And if you
grand - child- ren
F (onE) Dm (onE) F G
say the word I could stay with
on your knee Ve - ra, Chuck and
C
you
Dave
D. C.
(3rd time to Coda)
(G7)
CODA
C
-four (Ho!)
F6 Ab7 C6 A7 D7 G7 C6
sf
sf

She Loves You

Words & Music: John Lennon & Paul McCartney

SUGGESTED REGISTRATIONS

Electronic Organs	Drawbar Organs
Upper: Fl. 16(or 8), Fl. 2, Picc. 2	Upper: 60 7600 006
Lower: Str. 8, Diap. 8	Lower: (00) 5544 220 (0)
Pedal: 8	Pedal: 4-(2)
Vibrato: On	Vibrato: On

E♭
Cm
Gm
you she's thinking-ing of and she told me what to say-i-yah. She says she
now she says she knows you're not the hurt-ing kind She says she
E♭
Cm
loves you and you know that can't be bad, Yes, she
A♭m
B♭7
1
D♭
B♭7
loves you and you know you should be glad,
2. She
2
B♭
Cm
F
Oo
She loves you yeh, yeh, yeh, she loves you yeh,

Verse 3. Know it's up to you, I think it's only fair,
Pride can hurt you too, apologise to her.
Because she (loves you etc....)

Lady Madonna

Words & Music: John Lennon & Paul McCartney

SUGGESTED REGISTRATIONS

Electronic Organs	Drawbar Organs
Upper: Flute 8', 4', String 8', 4'	Upper: 55 8876 432
Lower: Diapason 8' String 8'	Lower: (00) 6504 033 (2)
Pedal: 16'+8'	Pedal: 5-(2)
Vibrato: On	Vibrato: On

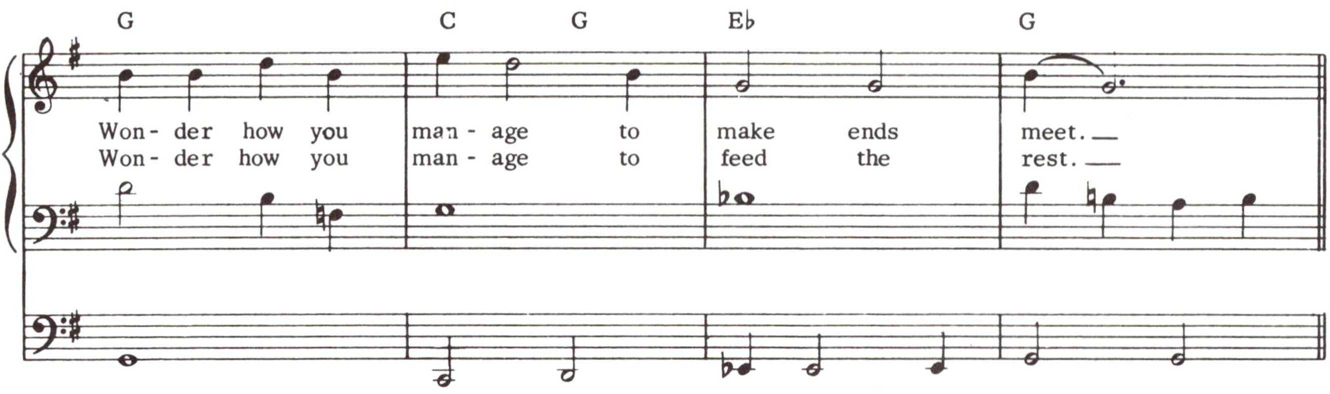

C
G
E♭
G
C7
mon-ey was heav - en sent? _
mu-sic play-ing in your head. _
Fri-day night ar - rives with-out a
Tues-day aft - er - noon is nev-er
F7
B♭
suit - case, _
end - ing, _
Sun-day morn-ing creep-ing like a
Wednes-day morn-ing pa-pers did-n't
Gm
C7
nun, _
come, _
Mon-day's child has learned to tie his
Thurs-day night your stock-ing need-ed
F7
B♭
Am
D7 sus 4
D7
G
C7
Repeat and fade
shoe - lace. See how they run. _
mend - ing.

I Want To Hold Your Hand

Words & Music: John Lennon & Paul McCartney

SUGGESTED REGISTRATIONS

Electronic Organs		Drawbar Organs	
Upper:	Flute 8', 4', 2' Mixt 2', String 8'	Upper:	40 6806 342
Lower:	Flute 8', 4' String 8	Lower:	(00) 5441 121 (0)
Pedal:	8'	Pedal:	4 - (2)
Vibrato:	On	Vibrato:	On

Medium beat

Upper

Lower

Pedal

C G7 Am

Oh yeh I'll___ tell you some-thing I think you'll un - der -
Please___ say to me___ you'll let me be your

Em C G7 Am Em

stand Then I'll ___ say that some-thing I wan-na hold your hand
man And please___ say to me___ you'll let me hold your hand

F G7 C Am (7) F G7 C

To Coda ⊕

1

— I wan-na hold your hand ___ I wan-na hold your hand. Oh___

C Gm7 C7 F
hand and when I touch you I feel hap-py in- side
Dm Gm7 C7 F G
It's such a feel - ing that my love I can't hide
mf
F G F G7
D. S. al Coda
I can't hide I can't hide Yeh
f
ff
CODA
F G7 E F G F C
I wan-na hold your hand I wan-na hold your hand
3
3

The Fool On The Hill

Words & Music: John Lennon & Paul McCartney

SUGGESTED REGISTRATIONS

Electronic Organs	Drawbar Organs
Upper: Diapason 8', Flute 8', 4'	Upper: 44 7657 432
Lower: Flute 8', String 8'	Lower: (00) 5444 333 (2)
Pedal: 8'	Pedal: 5-(2)
Vibrato: On	Vibrato: On

C
Am
F
G7
see that he's just a fool, And he nev - er gives an an - swer,
sound he ap-pears to make, And he nev - er seems to no - tice,
tell what he wants to do, And he nev - er shows his feel -ings
But the
Cm
Fm
Cm
B♭7sus
fool on the hill sees the sun go - ing down, And the
A♭9(♭5)
G7
eyes in his head see the world spinning
1 2
C
Dm7
'round.
3
C
'round.

Can't Buy Me Love

Words & Music: John Lennon & Paul McCartney

SUGGESTED REGISTRATIONS

Electronic Organs	Drawbar Organs
Upper: Clarinet 8', String 8', 4'	Upper: 00 8860 504
Lower: Diapason 8', Melodia 8'	Lower: (00) 6555 432 (0)
Pedal: 8'	Pedal: 5-(3)
Vibrato: On	Vibrato: On

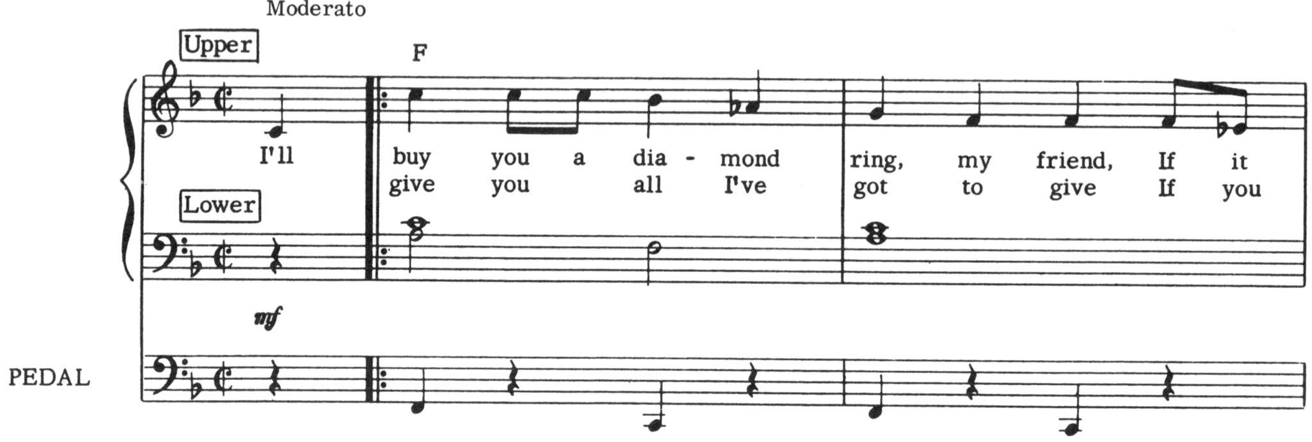

C7
Bb7
I don't care too much for mon - ey, For mon - ey can't buy me
1.
2.
F
love. 2. I'll
F
love. Can't buy me
Am
Dm
love,
F
Ev - 'ry - bod - y tells me so. Can't buy me
Am
Dm
love,
Gm7
C7
F
No, no, no, no!
3. Say you don't need no dia- mond ring And

F
Bb7
I'll be sat - is - fied. Tell me that you want those
F
C7
kind of things that mon - ey just can't buy, For I don't care too
Bb7
F
Am
Dm
much for mon-ey, For mon-ey can't buy me love. Can't buy me love,
Am
Dm
Gm7
C7
F
love. Can't buy me love!

Ticket To Ride

Words & Music: John Lennon & Paul McCartney

SUGGESTED REGISTRATIONS

Electronic Organs	Drawbar Organs
Upper: Flute 16', 8', 4' Trumpet 8'	Upper: 00 8768 007
Lower: Flute 8', 4', Diapason 8'	Lower: (00) 6446 432 (0)
Pedal: 16'+8'	Pedal: 5-(3)
	Vibrato: On

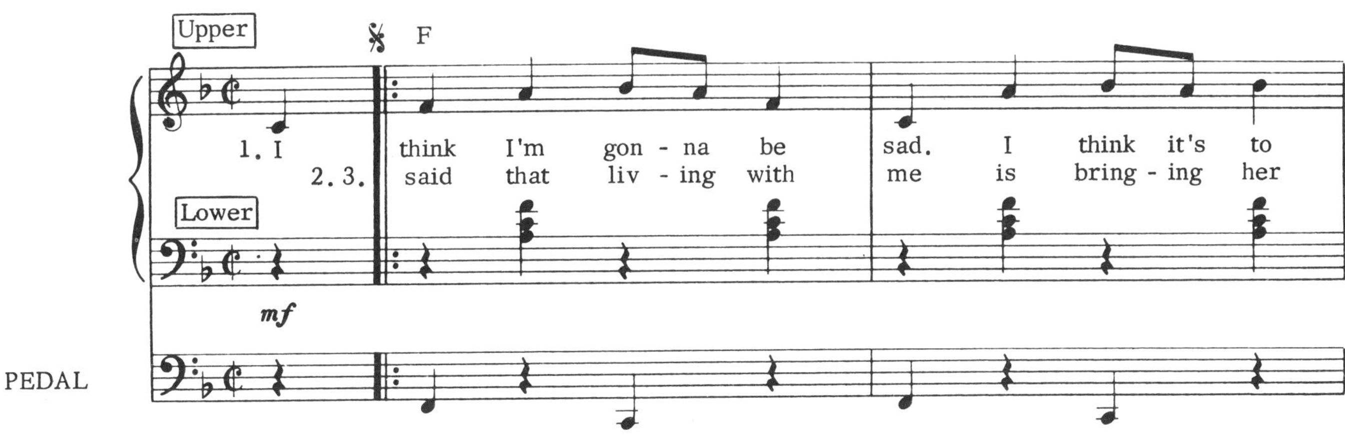

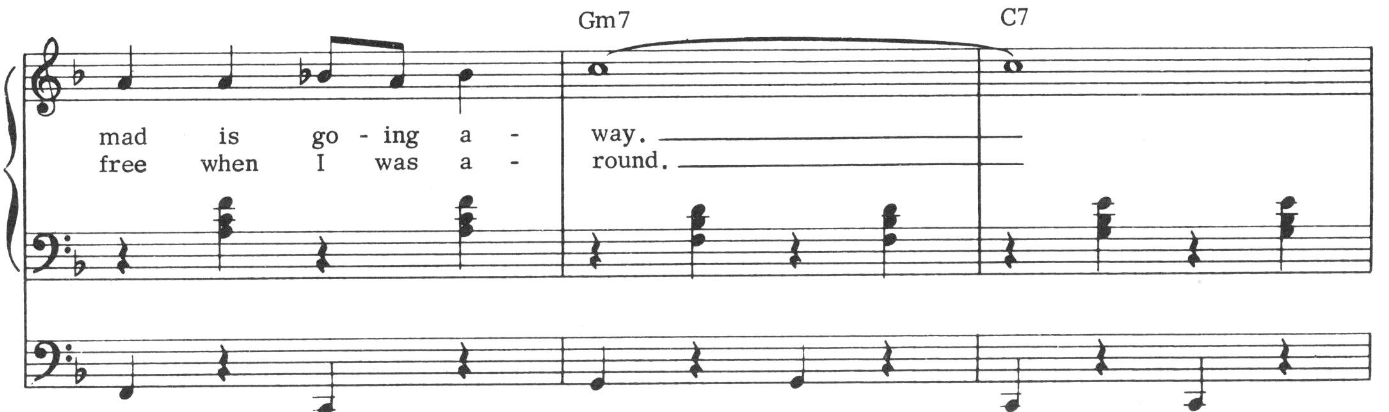

Dm
B♭
Dm
She's got a tick - et to
ride, ___
She's got a tick - et to
E♭
Dm
C7
ri - hi - hide,
She's got a tick - et to
ride, but she don't
to Coda
F
1.
2.
care. ___
2. She
I
B♭7
don't know why she's rid - ing so
high ___ She ought to

C
think right, She ought to do right by me. Be -

B♭7
fore she gets to say - ing good bye, ___ She ought to

C
C7
D. S. 𝄋 al Coda
think right, She ought to do right by me. 3. She

Coda
Repeat and fade
My ba - by don't care. My ba - by don't

Eight Days A Week

Words & Music: John Lennon & Paul McCartney

SUGGESTED REGISTRATIONS

Electronic Organs

Upper: Flute 8', String 8', Flute 4'

Lower: Diapason 8', French Horn 8'

Pedal: 16' and 8'

Vibrato: On

Drawbar Organs

Upper: 43 8070 604

Lower: (00) 4564 331

Pedal: 5-(4)

Vibrato: On

Moderato

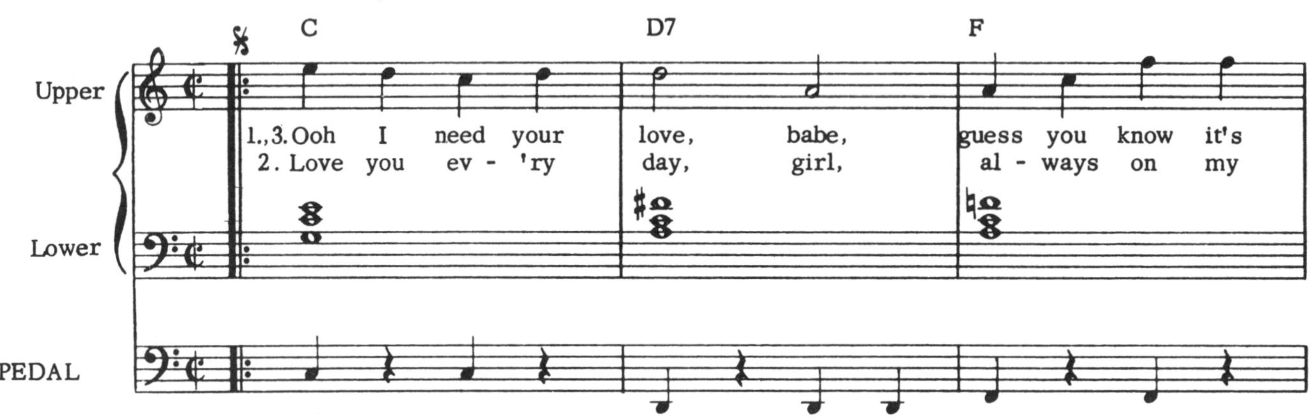

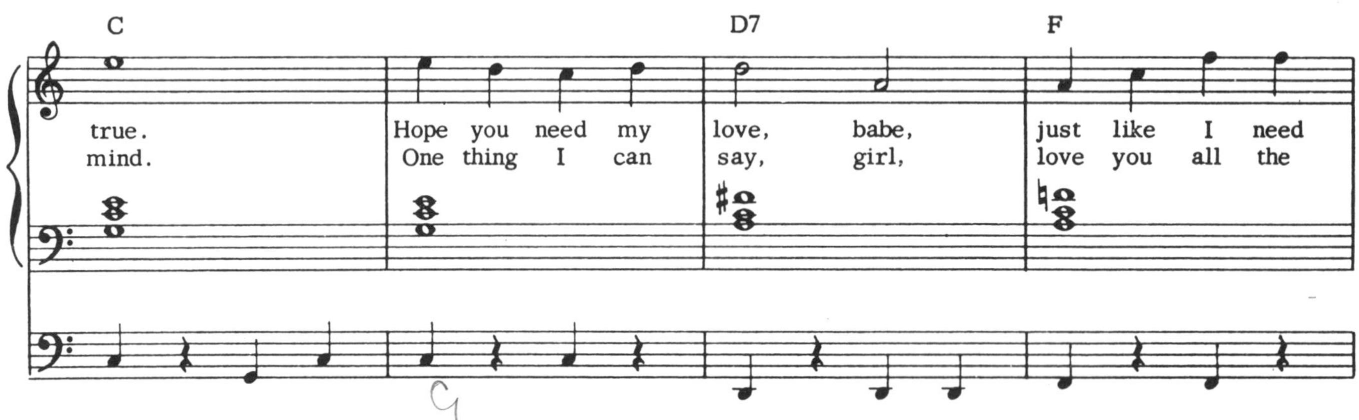

D7
C
D7
2nd time
to Coda
F
love me.
love me.
Ain't got noth- in' but
love, babe,
Eight days a
1.
C
2.
C
G
week.
week.
Eight days a
week I
Am
D7
love
you.
Eight days a
week is
F
G7
D.S. al Coda
not e- nough to
show I care.
Coda
F
C
Repeat and fade
Eight days a
week.

Yellow Submarine

Words & Music: John Lennon & Paul McCartney

SUGGESTED REGISTRATIONS

Electronic Organs		Drawbar Organs	
Upper:	Full Organ (16'-8')	Upper:	60 7755 444
Lower:	Diapason 8', String 8' French Horn 8'	Lower:	(00) 6644 323 (0)
Pedal:	16'+8'	Pedal:	5-(4)
Vibrato:	On	Vibrato:	On

March tempo

G
yel - low sub - ma - rine,
yel - low sub - ma - rine.
We all live in a
D
yel - low sub - ma - rine,
yel - low sub - ma - rine,
G
yel - low sub - ma - rine.
And our
As we
D
C
G
Em7
Am
C
friends are all on board, Man - y more of them live next
live a life of ease, Ev - 'ry one of us has all we
D
G
D
C
1.
G
2.
G
D. S. 𝄋
and fade
door And the band be - gins to play.
need Sky of blue and sea of green.

I Wanna Be Your Man

Words & Music: John Lennon & Paul McCartney

SUGGESTED REGISTRATIONS

Electronic Organs		Drawbar Organs	
Upper:	Flute 8', 4', Trumpet 8' Quint, Nazard	Upper:	72 7877 648
Lower:	Flute 8', 4' Diapason 8', Bassoon 8'	Lower:	(00) 8765 333 (0)
Pedal:	16+8	Pedal:	6-(4)
Vibrato:	On	Vibrato:	On

Moderate beat tempo

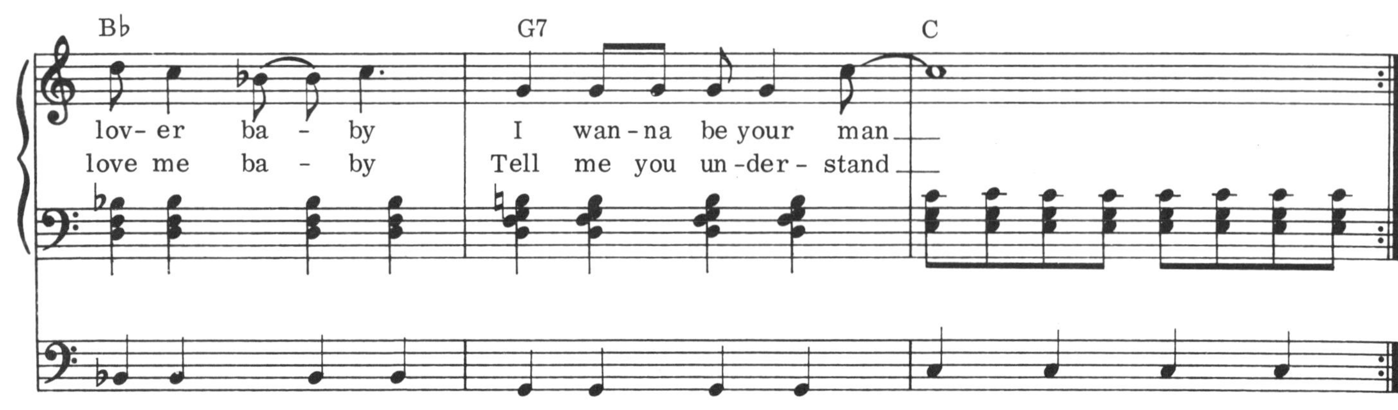

D7
G7
I wan-na be your man
C
(maj7)
(7)
A7
To Coda
C7
D.S. (with repeat) al Coda
CODA
(Repeat & fade)
man

Paperback Writer

Words & Music: John Lennon & Paul McCartney

SUGGESTED REGISTRATIONS

Electronic Organs	Drawbar Organs
Upper: Flute 8', 4', String 8'	Upper: 43 8070 604
Lower: Diapason 8', French Horn 8'	Lower: (00) 4564 331 (0)
Pedal: 16'+8'	Pedal: 5-(4)
Vibrato: On	Vibrato: On

Bright Rock

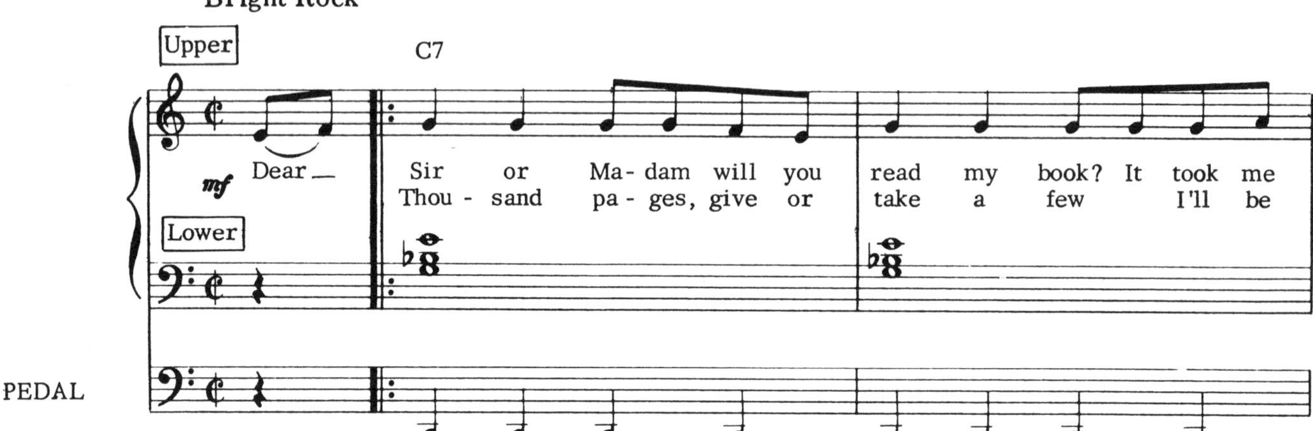

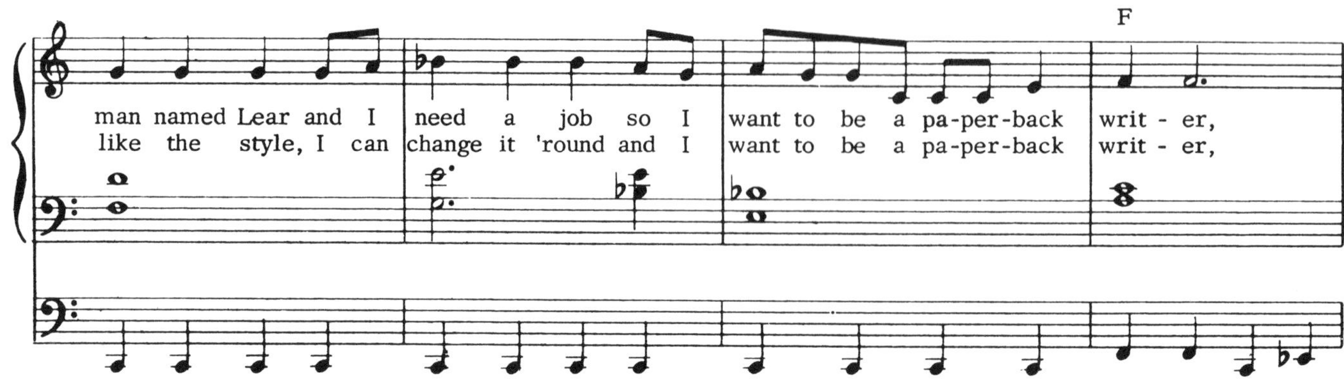

F C Bb C C7
pa-per-back writ - er. It's the dir - ty sto-ry of a
pa-per-back writ - er. If you real - ly like it you can
dir - ty man, and his cling - ing wife does-n't un - der-stand. His son is work-ing for the
have the rights, It could make a mil-lion for you o - ver night. If you must re - turn it you can
F
Dai - ly Mail; It's a stead - y job, but he wants to be a pa-per-back writ - er,
send it here, But I need a break and I want to be a pa-per-back writ - er,
C Bb C
1. 2.
pa-per- back writ - er. 2. It's a
pa-per - back writ - er.

Let It Be

Words & Music: John Lennon & Paul McCartney

SUGGESTED REGISTRATIONS

Electronic Organs	Drawbar Organs
Upper: Flute 16', 8', 4', Quint	Upper: 75 8846 003
Lower: Flute 8', String 8'	Lower: (00) 6554 321 (0)
Pedal: 16'+8'	Pedal: 5-(3)
Vibrato: On	Vibrato: On

Slow tempo

Upper

Lower

PEDAL

G D Em D C

1. When I find my-self in times of trou-ble Moth-er Ma-ry comes to me,
2. (And) when the bro-ken heart-ed peo-ple liv-ing in the world a-gree
3. (And) when the night is cloud-y there is still a light that shines on me,

G D C G D

Speak-ing words of wis-dom, let it be. And in my hour of dark-ness she is
There will be an an-swer, let it be. For tho' they may be part-ed there is
Shine un-til to-mor-row, let it be. I wake up to the sound of mu-sic

Em D C G D

stand-ing right in front of me, Speak-ing words of wis-dom, let it
still a chance that they will see, There will be an an-swer, let it
Moth-er Ma-ry comes to me, Speak-ing words of wis-dom, let it

C G Em D C G
be.
be. Let it be, let it be, let it be, let it be. Yeah
be.
Em D
1. C G
2. C G
Whis-per words of wis-dom, let it be. 2. And
There will be an an-swer, let it be. Let it
There will be an an-swer, let it
Em D C G D C G
be, let it be, let it be, let it be, Whis-per words of wis-dom, let it be.
to Coda
D.S. al Coda
C G D C G C G D C G
Coda
D C G

Yesterday

Words & Music: John Lennon & Paul McCartney

SUGGESTED REGISTRATIONS

Electronic Organs	Drawbar Organs
Upper: Flute 8', String 8'	Upper: 23 8776 558
Lower: Diapason 8', Flute 4'	Lower: (00) 7817 235 (0)
Pedal: 16'+8'	Pedal: 4-(4)
Vibrato: On	Vibrato: On

I be - lieve in yes - ter - day. Sud - den - ly
Dm G B♭ F
I'm not half the man I used to be, There's a shad - ow hang - ing
Em7 A7 Dm Dm7 B♭ C7
ov - er me; Oh, yes - ter - day came sud - den - ly.
F Dm G B♭ F
Why she had to go I don't know, she would - n't say,
Upper
Lower
Em7 A7 Dm B♭ Gm C7 F

Em7 A7 Dm Bb Gm C7 F
I said some-thing wrong, now I long for yes-ter-day.
Em7 A7 Dm Bb Gm C7 F
Em7 A7 Dm
Yes-ter-day, love was such an eas-y game to play,
Em7 A7 Dm Dm7
Bb C7 F C Dm G
Now I need a place to hide a-way; Oh, I be-lieve in
Bb C7 F C Dm G
Bb F G Bb F
yes-ter-day.
Lower Mm mm mm mm mm.
Vib: on
Bb F G Bb F

Eleanor Rigby

Words & Music: John Lennon & Paul McCartney

SUGGESTED REGISTRATIONS

Electronic Organs	Drawbar Organs
Upper: String 8', Flute 4'	Upper: 00 8768 553
Lower: Flute 8', (Or Melodia 8')	Lower: (00) 6543 333 (3)
Pedal: 16'+8'	Pedal: 6-(4)
Vibrato: On	Vibrato: On

Moderately

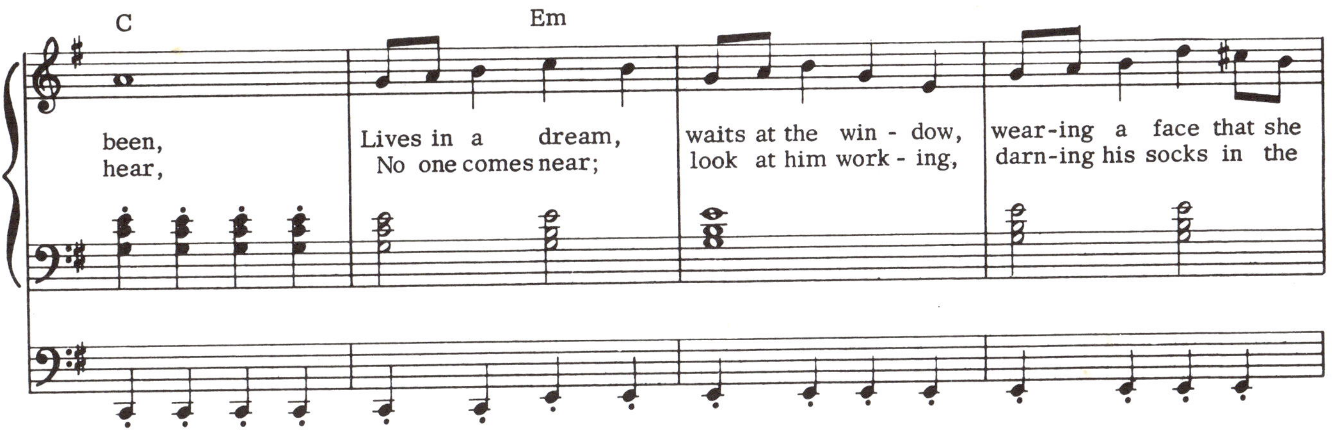

C
Em
keeps in a jar by the door.
night when there's no - bod - y there.
Who is it for?
What does he care?
All the lone - ly
C
Em
peo- ple, Where do they all come from?
All the lone - ly peo - ple, Where
C
1.
Em
2.
Em
C
do they all be - long?
long?
Ah, look at all the lone - ly
Em
Em
peo - ple
El- ea- nor Rig - by died in the church and was

C
Em
buried along with her name,
Nobody came.
Father McKenzie
C
Em
wiping the dirt from his hands as he walks from the grave,
No one was saved.
C
Em
All the lonely people, Where do they all come from?
C
Em
All the lonely people, Where do they all belong?
rit.

Norwegian Wood

Words & Music: John Lennon & Paul McCartney

SUGGESTED REGISTRATIONS

Electronic Organs	Drawbar Organs
Upper: Flute 16', 8', 4'	Upper: 75 8846 543
Lower: Flute 8', String 8'	Lower: (00) 6554 333 (2)
Pedal: 16'+8'	Pedal: 6-(3)
Vibrato: On	Vibrato: On

Gm
Wood? She asked me to stay and she told me to sit an - y where.
bed." she told me she worked in the morn - ing and start - ed to laugh.
C
Gm
So I looked a - round and I no - ticed there was - n't a chair.
I told her I did - n't and crawled off to sleep in the bath.
Am7
1. 2.
D7
G
Wood?
rit.

Help

Words & Music: John Lennon & Paul McCartney

SUGGESTED REGISTRATIONS

Electronic Organs	Drawbar Organs
Upper: Clarinet 8', String 4'	Upper: 00 8860 504
Lower: Melodia 8', Diapason 8'	Lower: (00) 6555 432 (0)
Pedal: 16'+8'	Pedal: 5-(3)
Vibrato: On	Vibrato: On

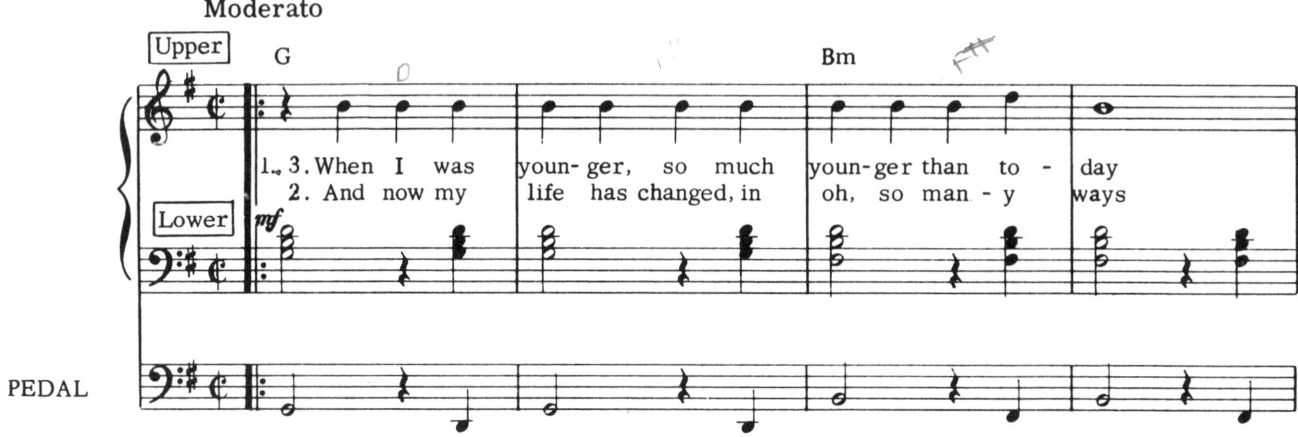

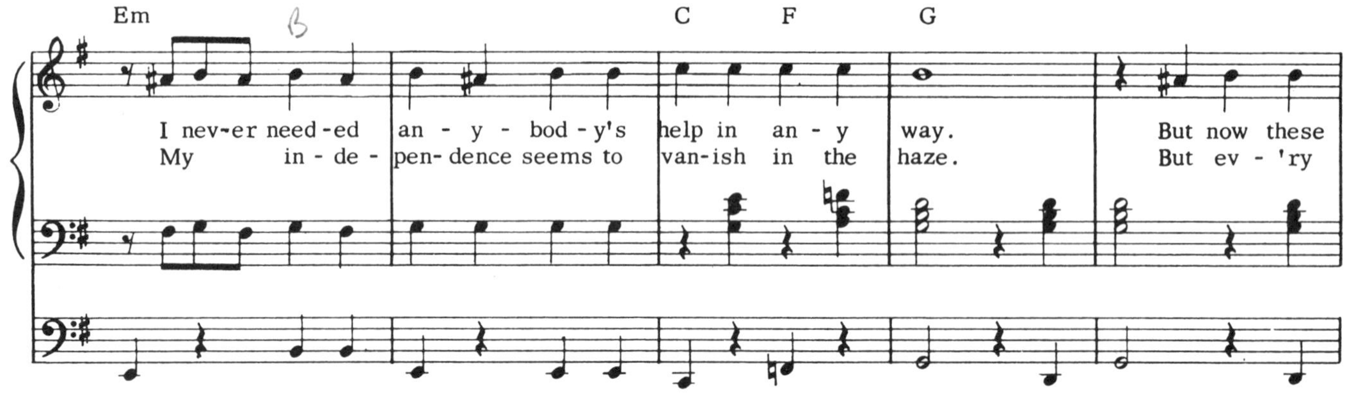

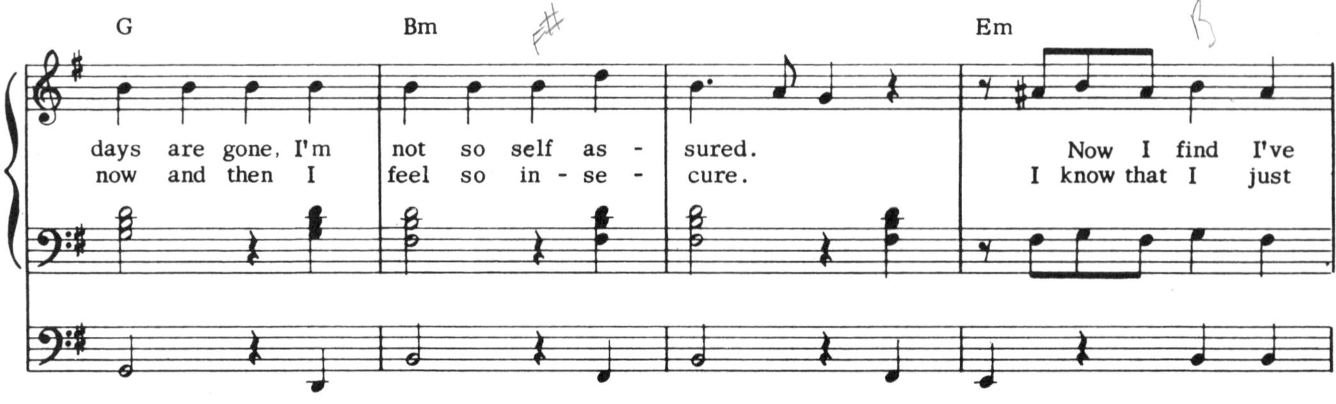

Em C F G Am
changed my mind, I've o-pened up the doors. Help me if you can. I'm feel-ing
need you like I've nev-er done be - fore.
Am F
down And I do ap-pre-ci - ate you be-ing 'round.
D7 G
Help me get my feet back on the ground. Won't you please,
1. 2.
3.
G Em G
please help me? me? Help me! Help me! Oo.

All You Need Is Love

Words & Music: John Lennon & Paul McCartney

SUGGESTED REGISTRATIONS

Electronic Organs	Drawbar Organs
Upper: Cello 16' (or Dulcian 16')	Upper: 75 8846 543
Lower: Flute 8', 4' (Melodia)	Lower: (00) 6554 333 (2)
Pedal: 16'+8'	Pedal: 6-(3)
Vibrato: On	Vibrato: On

Moderato

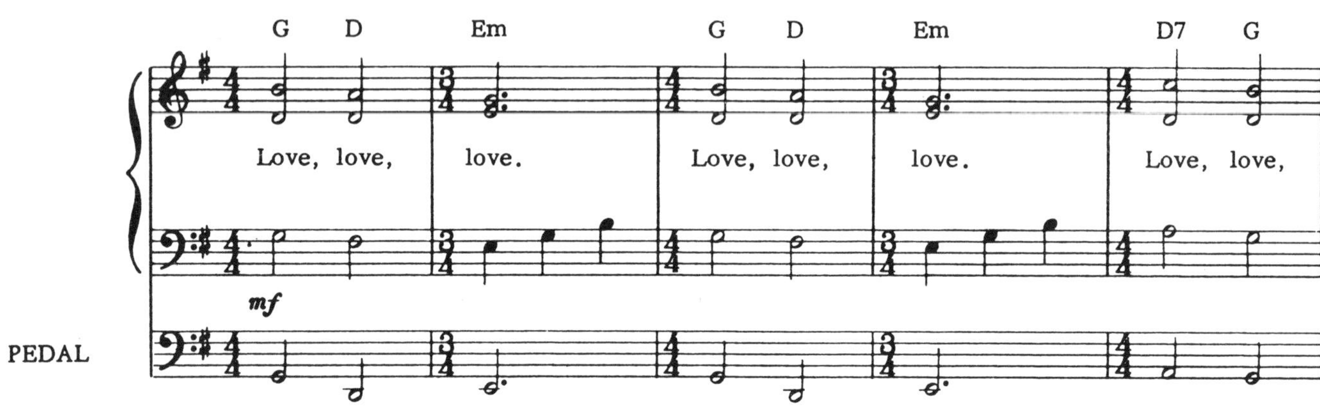

D7
G
3
D7
Noth - ing you can say, but you can learn how to play the game.
Noth - ing you can do, but you can learn how to be you in time.
No-where you can be, that is - n't where you're meant to be.
It's
easy
G
Am7
D7
All you need is love,
G
Am7
D7
All you need is love,
G
B7
All you need is
Em
G
love, love, —
C
D7
That is all you need
G
love.
D. C. last time
D. S. and fade

With A Little Help From My Friends

Words & Music: John Lennon & Paul McCartney

SUGGESTED REGISTRATIONS

Electronic Organs	Drawbar Organs
Upper: Full Swell (with 16')	Upper: 72 7877 648
Lower: Diapason 8' Flute 8', String 8'	Lower: (00) 8765 443 (0)
Pedal: 16'+8'	Pedal: 6-(4)
Vibrato: On	Vibrato: On

Moderato

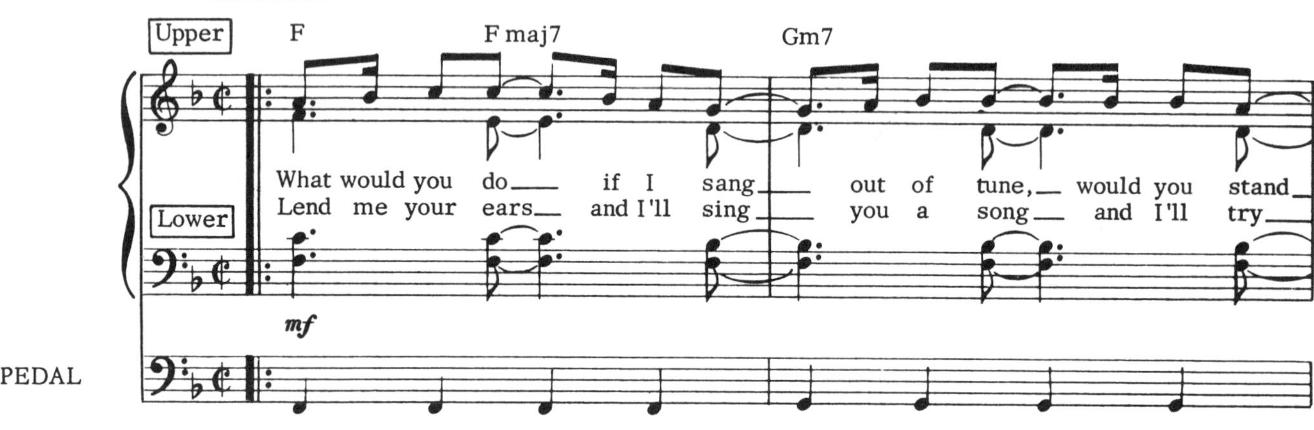

Eb Bb F
with a lit - tle help from my friends. Mm, I'm gon - na
Bb F Dm7
try with a lit - tle help from my friends. Do you need an - y
G7 F Eb Bb
bod - y? I need some - bod - y to love. Could it
Dm7 G7 F Eb Bb F
be an - y - bod - y? I want some-bod-y to love.

Strawberry Fields Forever

Words & Music: John Lennon & Paul McCartney

SUGGESTED REGISTRATIONS

Electronic Organs	Drawbar Organs
Upper: Flute 16', 4', Clarinet 8'	Upper: 00 8768 527
Lower: Diapason 8' French Horn 8'	Lower: (00) 5446 444 (0)
Pedal: 16'+8'	Pedal: 5-(3)
Vibrato: On	Vibrato: On

Correction Vibrato:

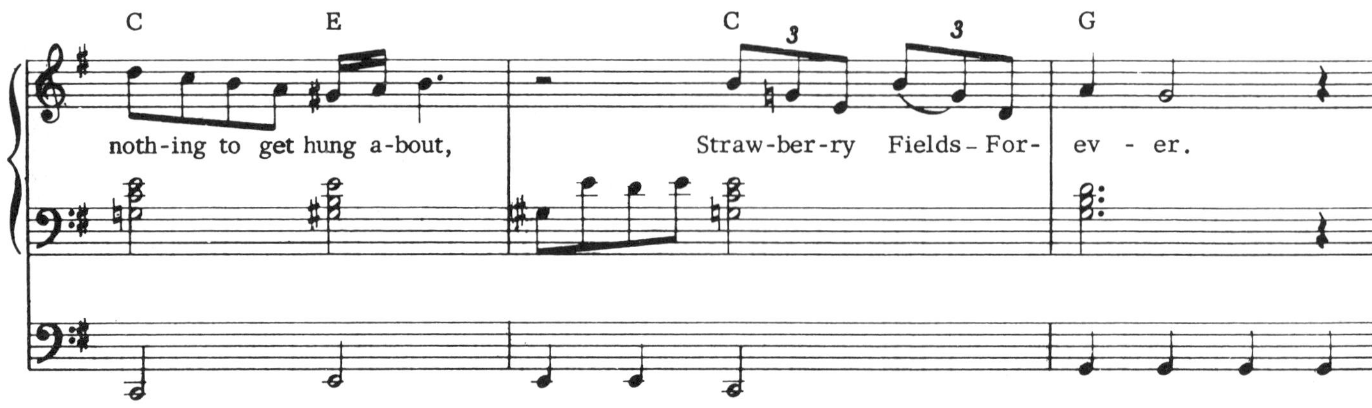

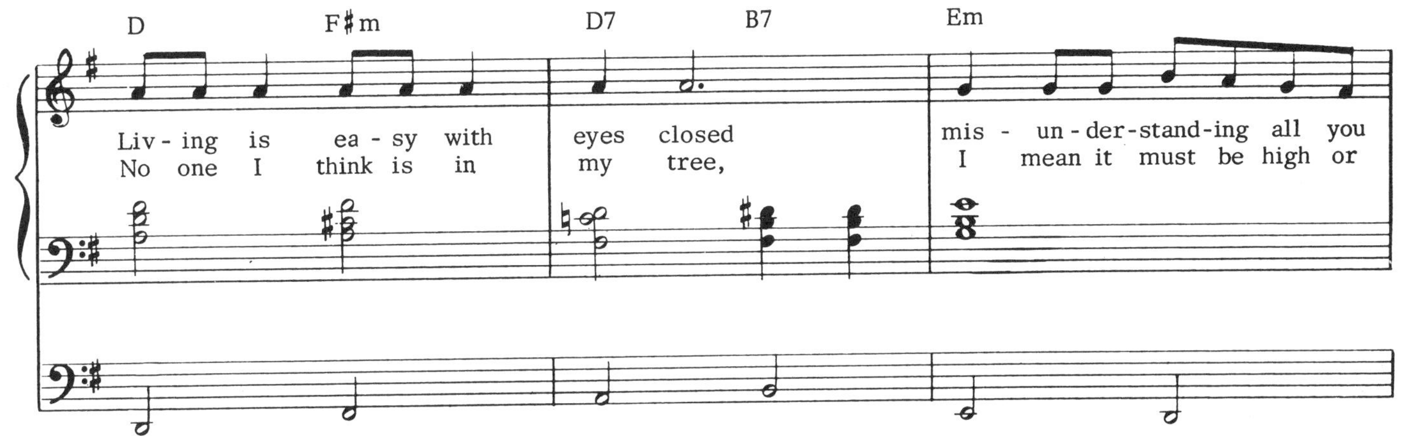
D F♯m D7 B7 Em
Liv - ing is ea - sy with eyes closed mis - un - der - stand - ing all you
No one I think is in my tree, I mean it must be high or

C D7
see. It's get - ting hard to be some -
low. That is you know you can't tune

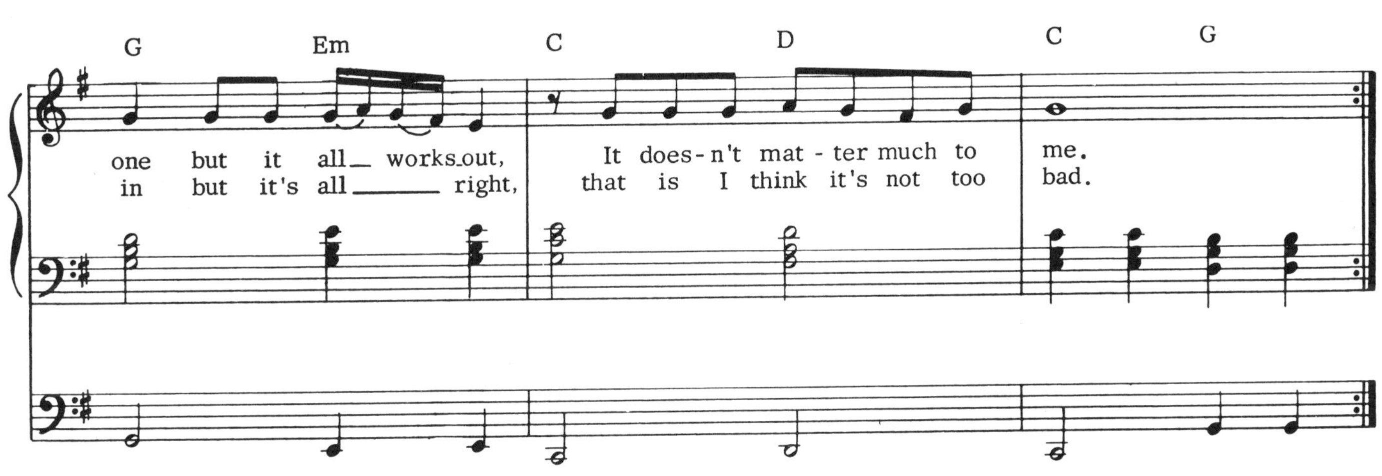
G Em C D C G
one but it all works out, It does - n't mat - ter much to me.
in but it's all right, that is I think it's not too bad.

G
Dm7
Let me take you down 'cause I'm go - in' to Straw - ber - ry
B dim
Fields. Noth - ing is real, and
C
E
noth - ing to get hung a - bout,
C
3
Straw - ber - ry Fields_ For -
G
C
G
ev - er, Straw - ber - ry Fields_ For - ev - er.

Penny Lane

Words & Music: John Lennon & Paul McCartney

SUGGESTED REGISTRATIONS

Electronic Organs	Drawbar Organs
Upper: Flute 16', 4' Clarinet 8'	Upper: 00 8768 527
Lower: Diapason 8',French Horn 8'	Lower: (00) 5446 444 (0)
Pedal: 16'+8'	Pedal: 5-(3)
Vibrato: On	Vibrato: On

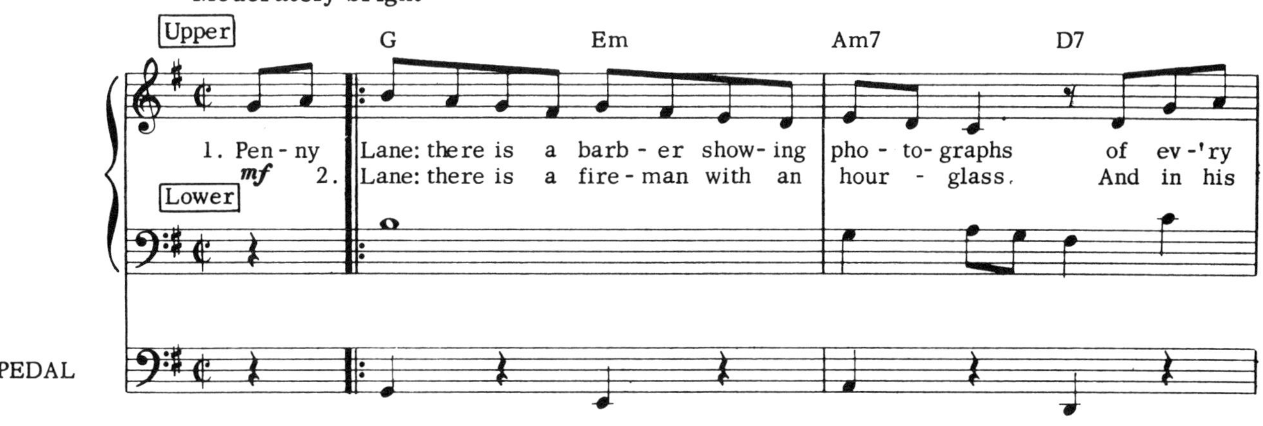

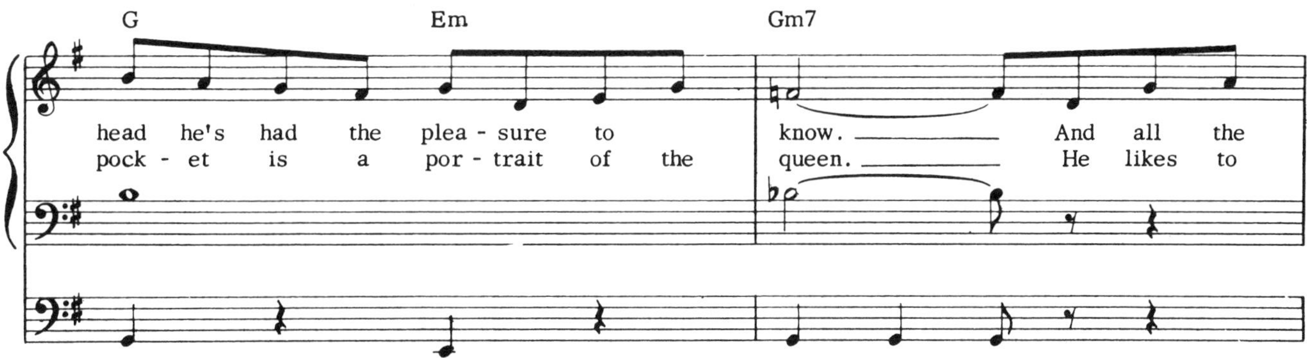

D7 G Em Am7 D7
On the cor-ner is a bank-er with a mot-or car. The lit-tle
Pen-ny Lane: the barb-er shaves an-oth-er cus-tom-er. We see the
G Em Gm7
chil-dren laugh at him be-hind his back. And the
bank-er sit-ting, wait-ing for a trend. And then the
Gm Eb D7
bank-er nev-er wears a "mac" in the pour-ing rain. Ver-y
fire-man rush-es in from the pour-ing rain. Ver-y
C F Am7 Bb
strange. Pen-ny Lane is in my ears and in my eyes.
strange.

Bb
F
Am7
Bb
Wet be-neath the blue sub-ur-ban skies I sit and
Wet be-neath the blue sub-ur-ban skies I sit and
1.
C dim
D7
mean-while 2. Back on Pen-ny
2.
C dim
D7
mean-while back.. Pen-ny
G
Lane is in my
Bm
ears and in my
C
eyes,
G
wet be-neath the
Bm
blue sub-ur-ban
C
skies
Pen-ny Lane!
G

Get Back

Words & Music: John Lennon & Paul McCartney

SUGGESTED REGISTRATIONS

Electronic Organs	Drawbar Organs
Upper: Flute 16', 8', 4'	Upper: 40 3446 556
Lower: Flute 8', String 8'	Lower: (00) 6420 000 (0)
Pedal: 16'+8'	Pedal: 5-(2)
Vibrato: On	Vibrato: On

Moderato

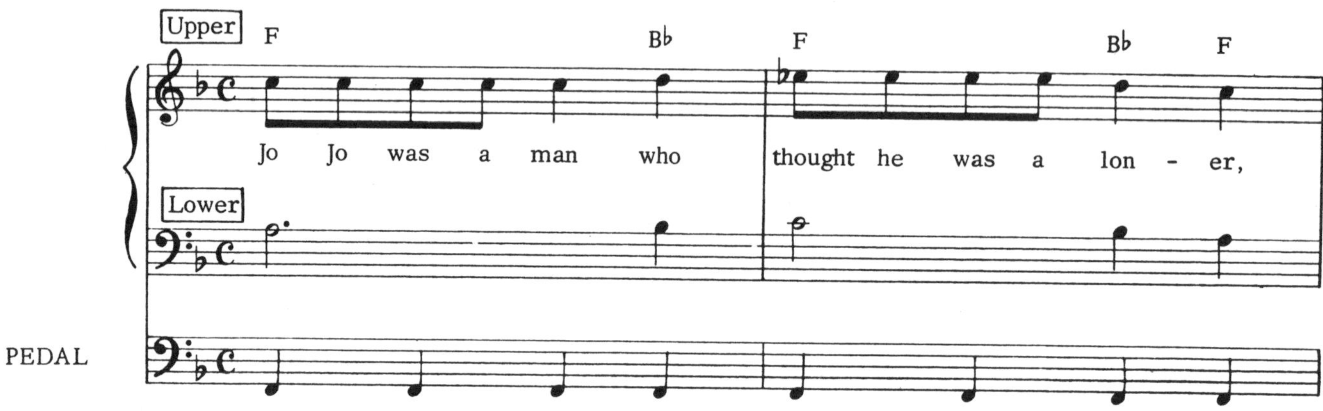

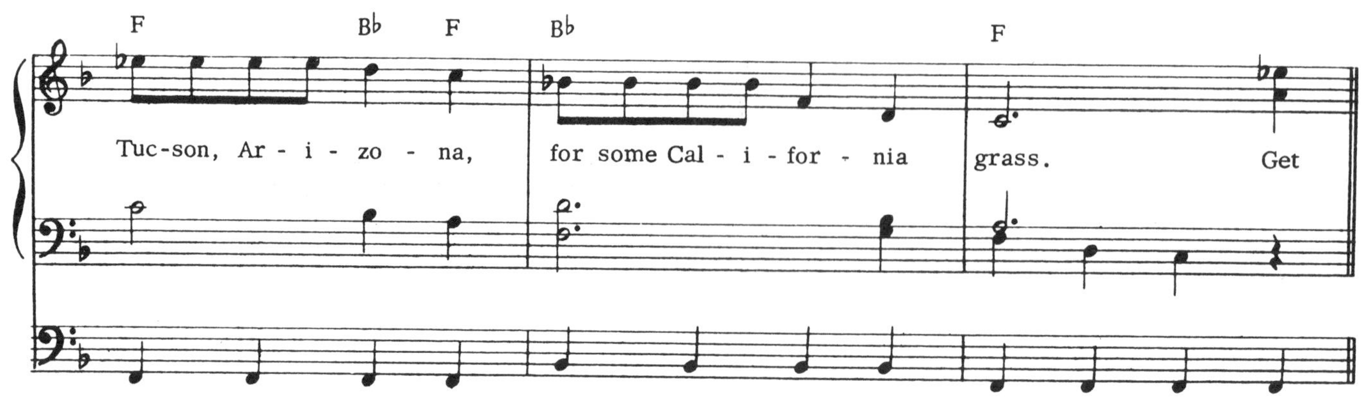

F7
Bb
Bb7
F
F7
back! Get back! Get back to where you once be - longed._ Get
Bb
Bb7
F
Fine
back! Get back! Get back to where you once be - longed._
F
Bb
F
Bb
F
Bb
F
Sweet Lor-et - ta Mod - ern thought she was a wom - an, But she was an-oth - er man.
Bb
F
Bb
F
Bb
F
D. S. al Fine.
All the girls a-round her say she's got it com - ing, But she gets it while she can. Get

Ob-La-Di, Ob-La-Da

Words & Music: John Lennon & Paul McCartney

SUGGESTED REGISTRATIONS

Electronic Organs	Drawbar Organs
Upper: Flute 16', 8', Clarinet 8'	Upper: 60 8000 804
Lower: Diapason 8', String 8'	Lower: (00) 6543 333 (0)
Pedal: 8'	Pedal: 5-(4)
Vibrato: On	Vibrato: On

F
F
Am
Dm
hand.
sing.
band.
Ob - la-
di, ob- la-
da, life goes
on
bra.
F
C7
F
1.
2.
D. C.
to 2nd Verse
3.
La la how the
life goes
on.
Ob - la -
Fine
In a cou-ple of
B♭
F
B♭
years they have
built a
home sweet
home with a cou-ple of
kids run - ning
D. C. to 3rd Verse
al Fine
F
C7
in the
yard of
Des - mond and
Mol - ly
Jones.

Michelle

Words & Music: John Lennon & Paul McCartney

SUGGESTED REGISTRATIONS

Electronic Organs	Drawbar Organs
Upper: Full Swell (with 16')	Upper: 72 7877 648
Lower: Diapason 8', Flute 8', String 8'	Lower: (00) 8765 443 (0)
Pedal: 16'+8'	Pedal: 6-(4)
Vibrato: On	Vibrato: On

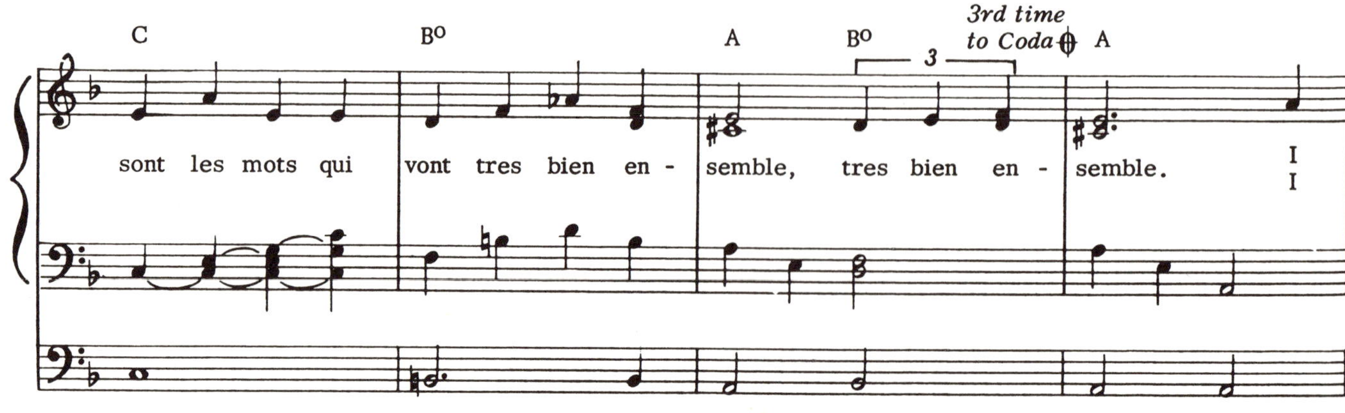

Dm
3
3
love you, I love you, I love you,
need to, I need to, I need to,
Cm
F7
Bb
That's all I want to say.
I need to make you see
A7
Dm
Gm
Dm
C# +
Dm7
Dm6
Un - til I find a way I will say the on - ly words I know that
Oh what you mean to me. Un - til I do, I'm hop - ing you will
Gm
A
D. S. al Coda
you'll un - der - stand.
know what I mean
Coda
A
Bb
semble. I will say the on - ly
Dm
Gm
A7
D
Gm
D
words I know that you'll un - der - stand, my Mi - chelle.
rit.

From Me To You

Words & Music: John Lennon & Paul McCartney

SUGGESTED REGISTRATIONS

Electronic Organs	Drawbar Organs
Upper: Flute 8', 4', String 8'	Upper: 43 8070 604
Lower: Diapason 8', French Horn 8'	Lower: (00) 4564 331 (0)
Pedal: 16'-8'	Pedal: 5-(4)
Vibrato: On	Vibrato: On

Medium tempo, with a beat

G7
C
G7
C
Em7
hold you and keep you by my side, I got lips that long to
A7
D7
D7+
G
kiss you and keep you sat - is - fied, If there's an-y-thing that you
Em
G
D7
C7
want, If there's an-y-thing I can do, Just call on me and I'll
Em
G
D7
D7+
G
send it a - long with love from me to you.

A Hard Day's Night

Words & Music: John Lennon & Paul McCartney

SUGGESTED REGISTRATIONS

Electronic Organs	Drawbar Organs
Upper: Flute 16' 4' Clarinet 8'	Upper: 00 8768 527
Lower: Diapason 8', French Horn 8'	Lower: (00) 5446 444 (0)
Pedal: 16'+8'	Pedal: 5-(3)
Vibrato: On	Vibrato: On

Moderately, with a beat

to Coda
C
F7
C
C
F
C
feel al - right. You know I work all day to get you
Bb
C
F
C
mon - ey to buy you things. And it's worth it just to hear you say you're gon-na
Bb
C
F
give me ev - 'ry thing. So why I love to come home 'cos when I
G7
C
F
C
get you a - lone you know I'll be o - kay. When I'm

Em
Am
Em
home
ev-'ry-thing seems to be al -
right,
When I'm
C
Am
Dm
G7
D. S. 𝄋 al Coda
home
feel-ing you hold-ing me
tight,
tight, yeah. It's been a
𝄌 Coda
C
F7
C
F7
C
F7
right,
You know I
feel
al -
right,
You know I
C
F7
B♭
C
feel
al -
right.

We Can Work It Out

Words & Music: John Lennon & Paul McCartney

SUGGESTED REGISTRATIONS

Electronic Organs	Drawbar Organs
Upper: Flute 8', 4' String 8'	Upper: 43 8070 604
Lower: Diapason 8' French Horn 8'	Lower: (00) 4564 331 (0)
Pedal: 16'+8'	Pedal: 5-(3)
Vibrato: On	Vibrato: On

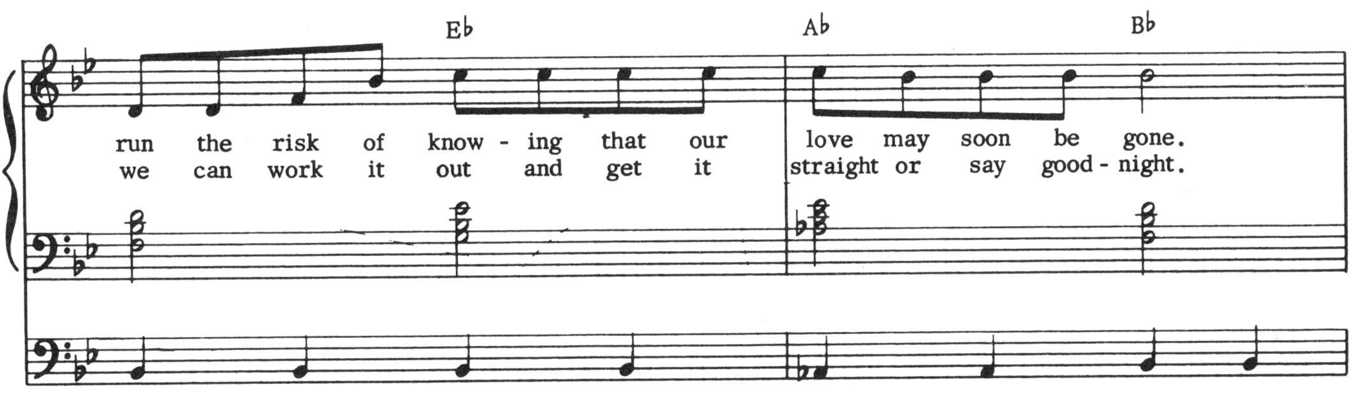

E♭ B♭ E♭ F7 Gm
We can work it out, We can work it out. Life is ver - y short
E♭ D7
and there's no time for fuss - ing and
Gm E♭ Gm
fight-ing, my friend. I have al-ways thought that it's a
E♭ D7 Gm E♭ Gm
crime so I will ask you once a - gain:

Bb
Eb
Bb
Eb
Try to see it my way,
on - ly time will tell if I am
Ab
Bb
Eb
Bb
right or I am wrong.
While you see it your way,
Eb
Ab
Bb
there's a chance that we might fall a -
part be - fore too long.
Eb
Bb
Eb
F7
Bb
Ab
Bb
3
3
We can work it out,
we can work it out.
rit.

Hello Goodbye

Words & Music: John Lennon & Paul McCartney

SUGGESTED REGISTRATIONS

Electronic Organs	Drawbar Organs
Upper: Clarinet 8' Flute 4'	Upper: 00 8060 050
Lower: Diapason 8', String 8'	Lower: (00) 4544 333 (2)
Pedal: 16'+8'	Pedal: 5 -(4)
Vibrato: On	Vibrato: On

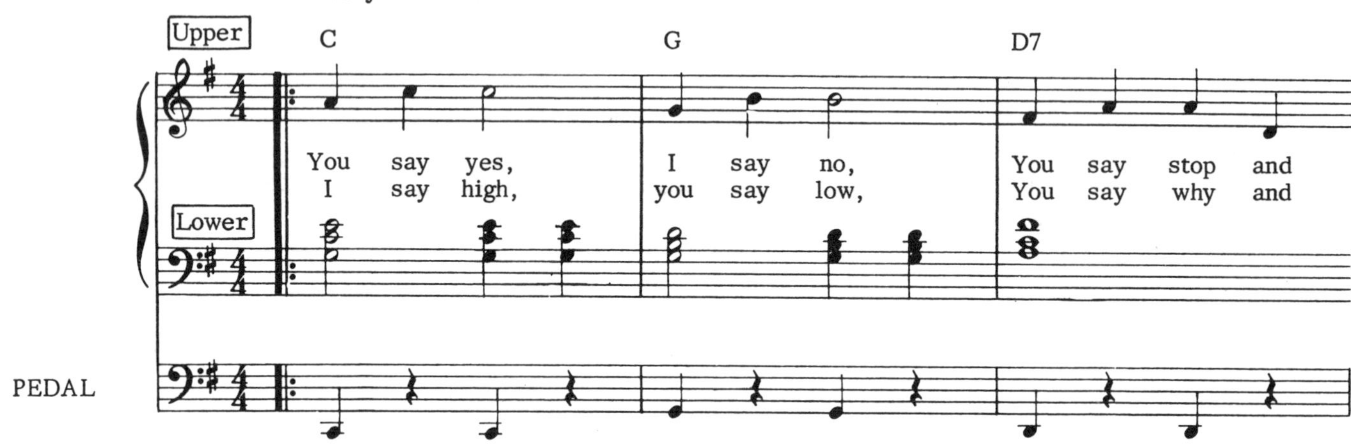

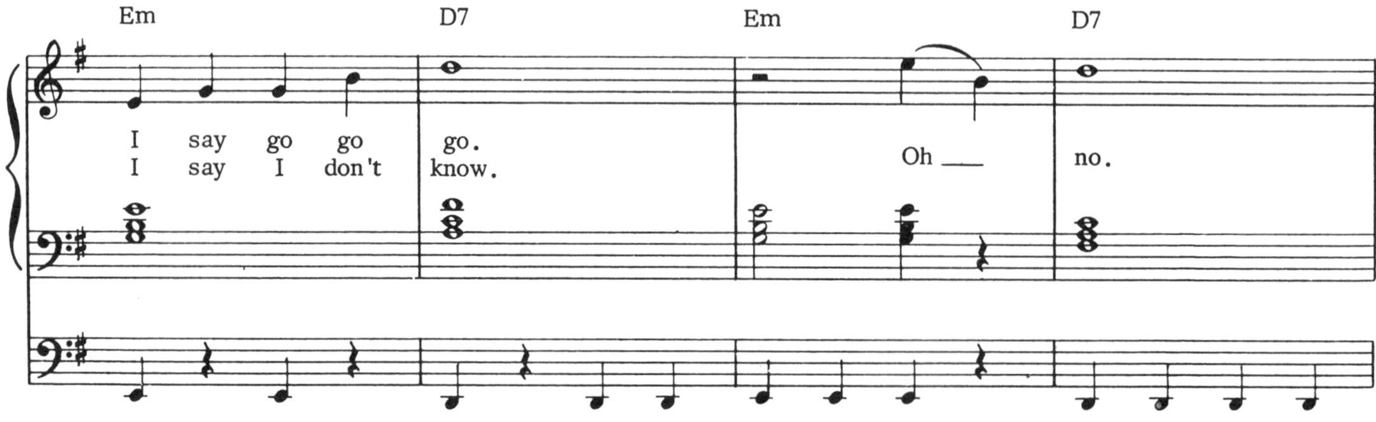

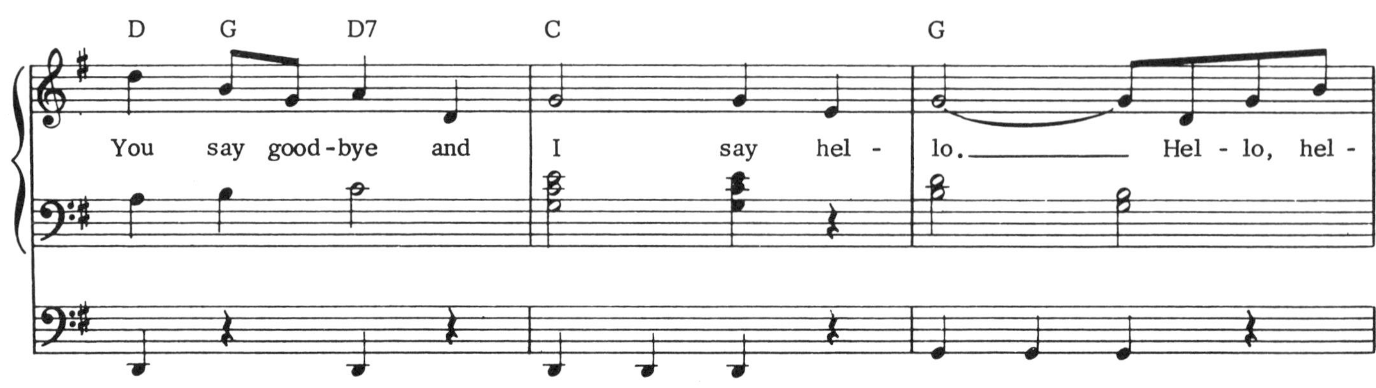

C
Eb
G
lo. I don't know
why you say good - bye, I say hel -
lo. Hel - lo, hel -
1.
C
F
G
lo. I don't know
why you say good - bye, I say hel -
lo.
2.
C
F
G
why you say hel - lo, I say good
bye. Hel lo, hel -
C
Eb
G
lo. I don't know
why you say good - bye, I say hel -
lo.

And I Love Her

Words & Music: John Lennon & Paul McCartney

SUGGESTED REGISTRATIONS

Electronic Organs		Drawbar Organs	
Upper:	Diapason 8', Flute 8'	Upper:	44 7657 432
Lower:	Horn 8', String 8'	Lower:	(00) 5444 333 (1)
Pedal:	16' and 8'	Pedal:	5-(2)
Vibrato:	On	Vibrato:	On

Moderately, with expression

2.
F
Dm
C
Dm
love her
A love like
ours
could nev - er
Am
Dm
Am
C7
die
As long as
I
have you
near me.
Gm
Dm
Gm
Dm
Gm
Bright are the
stars that shine,
Dark is the
sky;
I know this
Dm
B♭
C7
F
D
love of mine
will nev-er
die
And I
love her.
rit.

Hey Jude

Words & Music: John Lennon & Paul McCartney

SUGGESTED REGISTRATIONS

Electronic Organs	Drawbar Organs
Upper: Flute 16', 8', 4'	Upper: 36 4756 675
Lower: Diapason 8' French Horn 8'	Lower: (00) 3557 535 (0)
Pedal: 16'+8'	Pedal: 5-(4)
Vibrato: On	Vibrato: On

1.
2.
start to make it better. Hey
gin to make it better.
C7 F F
And any-time you feel the pain Hey Jude, re-
F7 B♭
frain, don't carry the world upon your
Gm7 C7
shoulders. For now you know that it's a fool
F F7

— who plays— it cool by mak - ing his world—
B♭
Gm7
— a lit - tle cold - er— Da da da da— da da da da
C7
F
C7
da
slight rit.
Hey
Jude,— don't let me
a tempo
F
down, You have found her— now go and get her.— Re -
C
C7
F

mem - ber to let her in - to your heart, then you can
B♭
F
start_ to make_ it bet - ter, bet - ter, bet - ter, bet - ter,
C7
F
bet - ter, bet - ter, Oh Da da da da da da da
F
E♭
da da da da Hey_ Jude. Jude.
B♭
F

Here There And Everywhere

Words & Music: John Lennon & Paul McCartney

SUGGESTED REGISTRATIONS

Electronic Organs	Drawbar Organs
Upper: Clarinet 8', Flute 4',	Upper: 00 8860 504
Lower: Diapason 8', Melodia 8'	Lower: (00) 6555 432 (0)
Pedal: 16'+8'	Vibrato: On
Vibrato: On	Vibrato: On

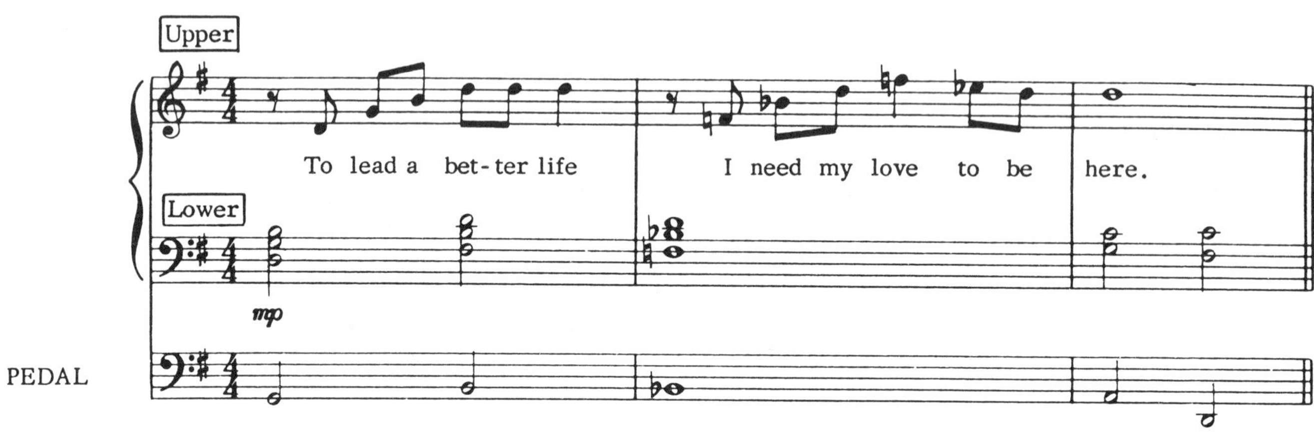

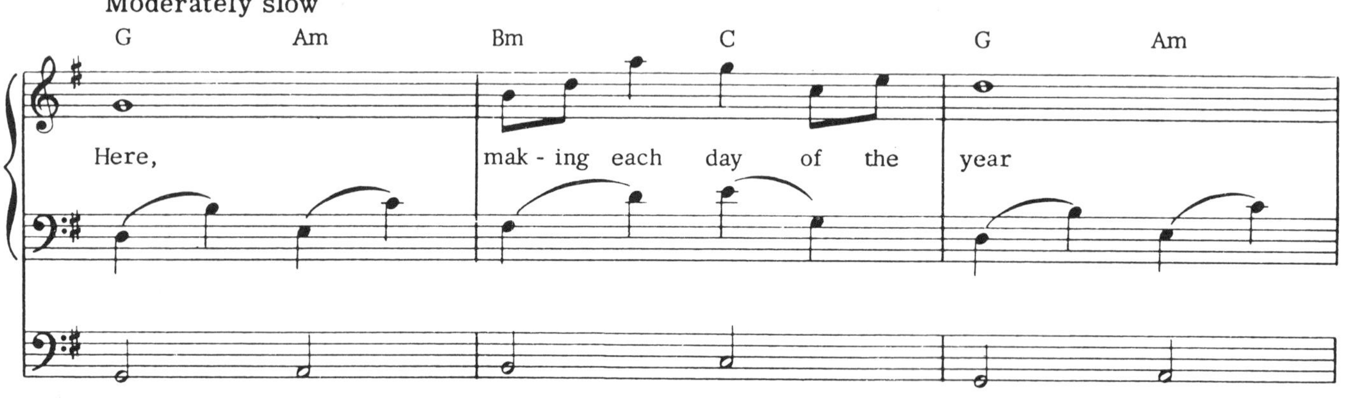

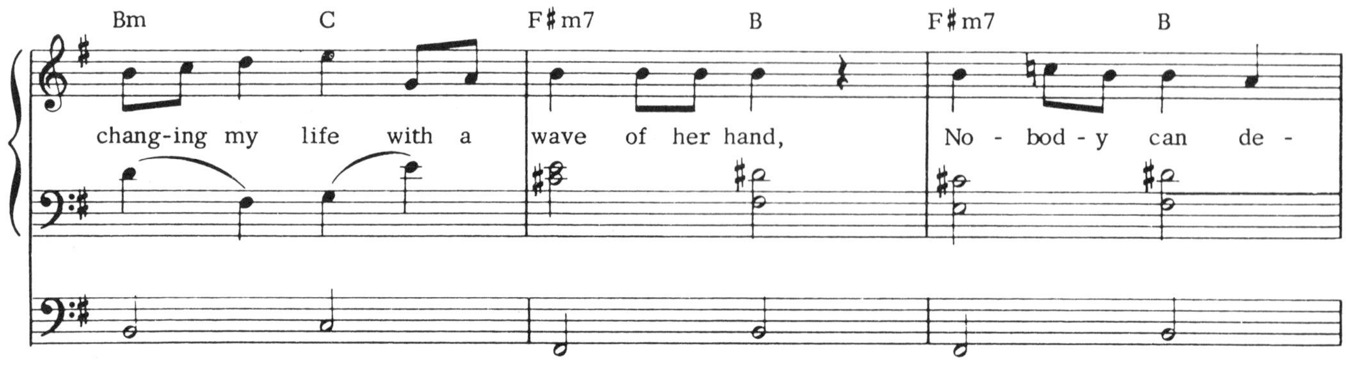

Em
Am
Am7
D7
G
Am
Bm
C
-ny that there's some-thing
there.
There,
run-ning my hands thru her
G
Am
Bm
C
F♯m7
B
hair,
Both of us think - ing how
good it can be;
F♯m7
B
Em
Am
Am7
D7
F7
Some - one is speak - ing, but
she does-n't know he's
there. I want her
B♭
Gm
Cm
D7
Gm
ev - 'ry - where and if
she's be-side me I know I need
nev- er care.
mf

11/86